OUR VOICES
SPANISH AND LATINO FIGURES OF AMERICAN HISTORY™

BERNARDO DE GÁLVEZ

SPANISH REVOLUTIONARY WAR HERO

MICHELLE MCILROY

rosen publishing's
**rosen
central**®

New York

Published in 2020 by The Rosen Publishing Group, Inc.
29 East 21st Street, New York, NY 10010

Library of Congress Cataloging-in-Publication Data

Names: McIlroy, Michelle, author.
Title: Bernardo de Gálvez : Spanish Revolutionary War hero / Michelle McIlroy.
Description: First edition. | New York : Rosen Publishing, 2020. | Series: Our voices: Spanish and Latino figures of American history | Includes bibliographical references and index. | Audience: Grades 5–8.
Identifiers: LCCN 2018006727 | ISBN 9781508184362 (library bound) | ISBN 9781508184355 (pbk.)
Subjects: LCSH: Gálvez, Bernardo de, 1746–1786—Juvenile literature. | United States—History—Revolution, 1775–1783—Participation, Spanish—Juvenile literature. | Governors—Louisiana—Biography—Juvenile literature. | Mississippi River Valley—History—Revolution, 1775–1783—Juvenile literature. | Florida—History—Revolution, 1775–1783—Juvenile literature. | Louisiana—History—Revolution, 1775–1783—Juvenile literature. | Gálvez, Bernardo de, 1746–1786—Juvenile literature.
Classification: LCC E269.S63 M43 2019 | DDC 973.3092 [B]—dc23
LC record available at https://lccn.loc.gov/2018006727

Manufactured in the United States of America

On the cover: Bernardo de Gálvez was a Spanish general who is remembered today as a Revolutionary War hero. Under his leadership, the Spanish forces and their allies were victorious over Britain.

CONTENTS

INTRODUCTION

Morning quiet was pierced by the sound of gunshots on April 19, 1775, when British troops faced American colonial militiamen in Lexington, Massachusetts. With these shots, a long-simmering conflict between Great Britain and American colonists boiled over into war. The American Revolution had begun. However, the real conflict had started long before; war doesn't begin in one day. American colonists were fighting to be heard, and their grievances against British rule started in the 1750s from conflict across the sea.

From 1754 to 1763, there was a war known in Europe as the Seven Years' War. This conflict spilled across all reaches of the powerful empires under Great Britain and France. The struggle took place on land as well as on the world's oceans. Great Britain and France were fighting for territory and global power. The strife affected Europeans in all parts of the world and other peoples in the colonies. In North America, this part of the fight was known as the French and Indian War, named for the British and Iroquois allies against the French military forces and the Huron. The American war centered around the claims of the Ohio and Mississippi River valleys. Both France and Great Britain wanted these lands for the sake of trade with their allies and expansion of territory.

In 1759, in the midst of this global upheaval, Spain's King Ferdinand VI died. Ferdinand VI had remained neutral in these conflicts, despite a long rivalry for control of the world's oceans and ports between Great Britain and Spain during the age of

Bernardo de Gálvez is remembered today for his heroic deeds during the Revolutionary War. His statue can be found in Washington, D.C.

exploration. Spain held a large empire in the New World, and the growing strength of the British Empire during the Seven Years' War concerned Spain. Would Great Britain threaten Spain's hold on the Americas and across the globe? When Ferdinand VI died, the rule passed to his half-brother Charles III, who was hungry to increase Spain's power in the world. In 1761, Spain renewed an old compact with France to provide support for France against Great Britain. With this, Spain's lands and wealth were brought into the growing conflict.

Britain defeated France in 1763. With the Treaty of Paris, France lost most of its territory to Great Britain, while signing the Louisiana Territory over to Spain. Great Britain took Florida from Spain. In addition, King George signed the Proclamation of 1763, stating that American colonists would not be permitted to settle lands west of the Appalachian Mountains, preserving these lands for the Native Americans to use. Colonists living in these areas would be forced to leave. The increased taxes demanded to pay for war, as well as this proclamation, would eventually trigger the American Revolution. At the same time, Spain would need to send powerful leaders into the Louisiana Territory to maintain control of their hard-won lands—and would eventually influence the fate of the American colonial struggle for independence. Bernardo de Gálvez, it would turn out, was the leader who would turn the tide for American patriots when they faced their own fight for freedom.

CHAPTER ONE

LIFE OF A LEADER

Bernardo de Gálvez was born July 23, 1746, in Macharaviaya, a village in the mountainous southern region of Málaga, Spain. Though his family wasn't royal, they were influential political figures in both Macharaviaya and beyond, with influence reaching all the way to New Spain in the Americas. His parents were Matías and Josepha Madrid y Gallardo de Gálvez.
Like his father, Bernardo attended a military science school named Academia de Ávila. After his education at the academy, Bernardo de Gálvez went on to serve in Spain's royal army.

Bernardo de Gálvez was born in Málaga, Spain. The Málaga region is a mountainous area found on the northern Mediterranean coast.

EARLY MILITARY CAREER

In 1762, when Bernardo de Gálvez was only sixteen years old, Spain invaded neighboring country Portugal as part of the Spanish royal pact with France to support their efforts in the Seven Years' War. This was Gálvez's first experience in military action, and it started his career as a lieutenant in the Spanish army. His work as lieutenant led to a promotion to captain of the Regiment of La Coruña.

Spain was growing an empire in the Americas. In 1765, Gálvez traveled to Spain's lands, in what is now Mexico, on military duty. He was part of an inspection alongside his uncle, José de Gálvez Gallardo. From there, he was given the responsibility of commanding troops in the northern frontier of New Spain. The borderlands of Sonora and Nueva Vizcaya were struggling from attacks by the Apache in that area. In 1769, Gálvez once again saw military action while trying to suppress these Apache attacks. While fighting along the Pecos and Gila Rivers, Gálvez was wounded two times. The Paso de Gálvez, on the Pecos River, is now named after Gálvez's crossing, where he led his troops to victory against the Apache.

After stabilizing the Sonora and Nueva Vizcaya region, Gálvez returned to Spain. He requested an assignment in France with the Regiment of Cantabria. With military and political ties between Spain and France, Gálvez decided to further his military training where he could also learn the French language and culture. This experience would be important to his future career in North America. After three years with this regiment in France, he returned to Spain and was posted to the Regiment of Seville. Just as revolution was erupting in North America, Charles III launched an invasion of the port city Algiers, in northern Africa,

THE LOUISIANA TERRITORY

During the conflict of the Seven Years' War, France needed support as it fought against Great Britain. In a secret agreement, called the Treaty of Fontainebleau, France gave a large territory in North America to Spain. France and Spain both dearly desired to keep lands and power away from Great Britain. Additionally, France hoped offering Spain territory would encourage Spain's economic and military support. This territory was the Louisiana Territory.

During the Seven Years' War, Spain gained control of the Louisiana Territory, stretching from the Mississippi River to the Rocky Mountains.

(continued on the next page)

(continued from the previous page)

The territory covered lands of the Mississippi River and its tributaries, stretching from the Gulf of Mexico to Canada and from the Mississippi River to the Rockies. Great Britain maintained the right to navigate the Mississippi River and held lands east of the river, while Spain was given control of the port city New Orleans and all territory west of the Mississippi in North America. The lands along the Ohio and Mississippi River valleys had already been explored by Great Britain, France, and Spain throughout the colonial era. France had an extensive fur trading network stretching from New Orleans to Canada that relied on the mighty Mississippi for transport of goods. The Proclamation of 1763 kept American colonists from establishing settlements along the eastern part of the Louisiana Territory. This angered colonists and weakened Great Britain's hold of the territory when Spain acquired it. It would exchange hands several times throughout the colonial period, until the United States purchased the entire Louisiana Territory from France, which once again held the territory, in 1803.

in hopes of punishing pirate activity that had stemmed from that area against Spain for years. Charles III needed to show the world Spain's military might as the unrest in the Americas grew. Instead of the brilliant success King Charles III hoped for, it was a disaster resulting in many losses for Spain's military. Gálvez survived but returned to Spain, seriously wounded from the failed invasion. He was promoted to lieutenant-colonel and spent time as a teacher in his former school, Academia de Ávila during his recovery.

LOUISIANA

In 1776, Gálvez was transferred to the Louisiana Territory. Fighting between the American colonists and Great Britain had already been underway for more than a year when Gálvez arrived in New Orleans, the capital of the Louisiana Territory. The colonies had declared independence from Great Britain, and Gálvez was arriving as colonel of a regiment at a time when Spain needed to keep strong control of the lands under Spanish rule in the Americas. As Great Britain struggled to hold on to its grasp on their territory, Spain could strengthen its own.

In 1777, Gálvez was promoted to governor, replacing Luís Unzaga y Amezaga. Amezaga had helped Louisiana make the transition from French control to Spanish government. It was up to Gálvez to continue this leadership, promote emigration from Europe to Louisiana, and further revitalize the economy of the territory. His official duty as governor began January 1, 1777. The time Gálvez had spent in France served him well once he moved to Louisiana, which had long been under French control. He was able to pass laws that encouraged Louisiana's colonists to trade with France and French colonies, boosting the economy and maintaining peaceful relations in the territory.

The year 1777 was an eventful one for Gálvez. He married Félicité de Saint-Maxent d'Estréhan after his arrival in Louisiana. She was born in Louisiana Territory to a wealthy and influential French military family. Her father was helpful to the community in the territory before and after they married. The married couple had three children: a son named Miguel and two daughters, Matilde and Guadalupe. As governor, he successfully brought

This ceramic plaque from Spain depicts Gálvez. He was promoted to the position of governor of the Louisiana Territory in North America in 1777.

trade and growth to the Louisiana Territory. However, the American Revolution was in full swing. Gálvez would soon be more than just an important governor in the eyes of the Spanish crown; he would become an instrument for changing history in the Americas.

CHAPTER TWO

SMUGGLER AND SPY

As the American Revolution unfolded, Spain witnessed the American colonists taking their first steps toward independence through acts of rebellion: the Boston Tea Party, fiery speeches by patriots like Patrick Henry, Thomas Paine's pamphlets urging freedom, and the fighting that broke out at Lexington and Concord. After the Declaration of Independence was signed in 1776, fighting spread. As the governor of the Louisiana Territory, Gálvez would play a key role in this war. His efforts to promote trade with the French helped both France and American colonial economies. The colonies needed an economy that didn't depend on Great Britain. Gálvez allowed American ships to use the Mississippi River for trade and distribution of goods and military supplies. At the same time, he blocked British ships from entering the port of New Orleans or sailing there. Governor Gálvez accused eleven British ships of smuggling goods and seized them. At the same time, he wrote a decree that the port of New Orleans would continue to be open to American trade, and capturing British ships would not be punished. Further, stolen British goods were allowed to be sold. The loss of the goods aboard these ships was costly for Britain. Gálvez was fulfilling his duties as governor and strengthening Spain, but his success helped the American colonies, too.

SMUGGLING AND SECRETS

To win freedom, the revolutionaries needed supplies, medicine, and secret ways to spread information and form strategies. In a time before computers and phones, sharing information meant carrying written letters and materials from one area of the rebellion to another without interception. As Spain became more involved, Gálvez oversaw a smuggling operation to support the colonies. One American leader at Fort Pitt received nearly

This sculpture of Oliver Pollock, by Frank Hayden, looks over the public library in Baton Rouge, Louisiana. Pollock and Gálvez worked together to support American revolutionaries.

$70,000 worth of supplies from this network. Through all of this, Gálvez himself managed to avoid capture by British spies, who were always present in New Orleans as the war unfolded. He continued to smuggle medicine, uniforms, weapons, and other supplies along the Mississippi River to the revolutionaries. He corresponded with Patrick Henry and promised to maintain supply lines to the American colonists. Gálvez and Thomas Jefferson were also in contact to direct supplies and messages along this important network.

Finally, Gálvez made contact with a wealthy Irish American patriot named Oliver Pollock. Pollock used his own wealth and worked with Gálvez to sneak supplies across the territory into the American colonists' hands. Pollock was labeled a traitor in the eyes of Great Britain, which was a crime punishable by death. British officials demanded that Gálvez turn Pollock over to them, but he refused. Through all of this—smuggling goods, contacting important Revolutionary figures, spreading military secrets, and controlling New Orleans for the benefit of the patriots—Gálvez was a key figure in the success of the American Revolution, and this was all before Spain officially declared war on Great Britain!

SPAIN ENTERS THE WAR

By 1779, the American Revolution was already four years underway. King Charles III of Spain saw the opportunity to strengthen his own boundaries in the Americas and potentially weaken Great Britain through this revolt. He had interest in taking back lands once held by Spain that had been lost to Great Britain in the Seven Years' War. However, King Charles III could see the risks of encouraging the colonists of any empire in revolution against their king. Instead of signing a treaty to

This portrait of King Charles III was painted by Anton Raphael Mengs in the mid-1700s. King Charles III saw the American Revolution as an opportunity to strengthen Spain.

become official allies of the colonies, he signed an alliance with France. By becoming allies with the colonists' allies, Spain was declaring war on Great Britain and strengthening the American patriots' chances of becoming independent.

Spain officially declared war on June 21, 1779. Gálvez was already working with the patriots to provide intelligence and supplies but would now need to further strengthen the

THE TALE OF TWO FLORIDAS

When the French and Indian War concluded with the Treaty of Paris in 1763, France lost nearly all of the territory it once held in North America. Spain wanted to regain Havana, which had been captured by Great Britain during the war. Havana was one of Spain's most important ports. To get Havana back, the treaty stated that Spain must give Great Britain Florida. All this was agreed upon in the treaty. When Britain gained Florida from Spain, it divided that territory into two separate colonies: East Florida and West Florida. East Florida was the area between the Apalachicola River, the Gulf of Mexico, and the Atlantic Ocean, or the peninsula we recognize as Florida today. The capital of this colonial territory was St. Augustine. Great Britain offered settlers land in this area to encourage farming and a growing population. Many loyalists moved there once the American Revolution began, seeking refuge from the war-torn areas in the Carolinas and the

(continued on the next page)

(continued from the previous page)

north. West Florida, with Pensacola as capital, stretched all the way to the Mississippi River in the west, along the Gulf Coast. The land in West Florida wasn't good farm-land, but could provide timber to the British. Being close to the Mississippi River and sitting on the Gulf Coast, Spain saw West Florida as a place to guard against inva-sion from Great Britain. If Spain captured West Florida, it could secure an important area of the continent for trade and protect New Orleans.

Mississippi against military action by Great Britain. Great Britain had enormous resources, war ships, and a strong presence in the southern colonies. It held East and West Florida, once claimed by Spain, which threatened Spain's security in the Gulf Coast and along the Mississippi River. Great Britain's immedi-ate response to Spain's actions was to make every effort to take New Orleans and the powerful Mississippi, which Gálvez and his allies knew would cripple their efforts to supply the American colonies with munitions and would crush the economy of the Louisiana Territory. Whoever controlled the Mississippi River controlled the continent beyond it. He also knew that any loss of Louisiana would threaten the rest of Spain's claims in the Americas. It would take brilliant strategy and the support of a diverse population to keep the life-line Mississippi open and free from British hands. As governor of the Louisiana Territory under the Spanish crown, Gálvez used his important connections to the French community as well as the patriots in the rest of Britain's colonies to protect New Orleans and the rest of the river for Spain.

CHAPTER THREE

HURRICANES AND RIVER CAMPAIGNS

W hen Spain joined the war in June 1779, King Charles III put Gálvez in charge of all Spanish troops in America. Gálvez knew he would need a strong militia to defend the Louisiana Territory against Great Britain. The skillful leader recognized that the upper-class citizens didn't want to march side by side with people they felt were less important. To convince people of all classes to join his militia, Gálvez created a special cavalry. With help from Pollock, this cavalry was dressed in fancy uniforms, complete with golden buttons for the upper class. In the French community, Gálvez used his marriage to the wealthy and important Félicité de Saint-Maxent d'Estrehan to

As Spain became involved in the American Revolutionary War, Gálvez used his skills as a leader and connections in Louisiana to defend Spain's territory.

encourage participation. He also recruited free black men to join a segregated militia with their own officers. Gálvez was a talented speaker. His inspiring speeches resulted in an army filled with men from all different backgrounds. Creek, Choctaw, Alabama and other Indians, Canary Islanders, French-speaking and Spanish-speaking colonists, upper-class men, working-class men, Irish Americans, Germans, and a black militia all served alongside this inspirational leader.

MILITARY FORTS

Military forts had been used to establish European power in the Americas since the age of exploration. Wherever a European empire attempted to settle, it was faced with opposition from the people already living there. Establishing trade and colonial settlements was impossible without a form of security. In Europe, forts had long been built to protect the interests of a country from invasion. These European forts were elaborately designed to allow maximum defense against any attempted invasion and often involved stone-work and trenches for defense. In the colonies, the first forts were often protected by stockade walls and earthen embankments instead. Fort Bute, for example, was shaped like a star and defended by earthen walls. Baton Rouge was another example of fortification in the colonial era. It was another earthen fort, but surrounded by a wide trench up to 9 feet (2.7

meters) deep. Beyond this trench was a tall stockade fence made of sharpened stakes. It would not be easy to attack such a fort on foot. The defenders inside were well protected by the thick earthen walls, deep trenches, and sturdy fencing all around. Many such forts existed in the Americas during this time period. Wherever trade posts were desired–along rivers, at the coastline, and other strategic places–forts were built. Some of these forts were more like protected villages than military outposts. Inside such places, such as Galveztown, Louisiana, a small village with houses, church, and plaza might be found. The villagers would be protected by a military presence and a stockade fence or other wall. Daily life in peaceful times could allow travel beyond the gates of the fortified village, but citizens could withdraw inside for protection in times of conflict. Many modern cities and towns along US rivers and shorelines grew near the influence of these centers of protection and trade. Some forts have been preserved for visitors and can give guests some idea of what life must have been like within their walls.

Many military forts found throughout North America used wooden stockades for defense. Forts dotted the Mississippi River and Gulf of Mexico coastline, which Gálvez fought to overtake.

Gálvez cared for his troops. He knew that the men marching for him, and for Spain, were mostly militia—not men who had made a military career—and that many had families to return to. To feed this army, Gálvez sent emissary Francisco García to Texas. There, García requested beef to be delivered to the Louisiana Territory to feed the men marching with Gálvez. Many cattle were rounded up and sent to Gálvez and his troops. Inspiring speeches, careful organization of special militia groups, freely sharing supplies with American troops, and feeding his men well all proved that Gálvez was a man worth fighting with.

SECURING THE MISSISSIPPI

With war on the doorstep, New Orleans was in immediate danger of attack. Spain needed to secure the port or lose control of the Mississippi and beyond. The now-promoted Brigadier General Gálvez gathered his troops to defend New Orleans in August 1779. Even as they gathered, a storm was brewing. As the fleet readied to defend the port, a hurricane struck. In less than a day, this massive storm flattened houses, destroyed food sources, and sank several ships. Some of Gálvez's troops drowned. Despite terrible damage, Gálvez knew he needed to press on if New Orleans and Louisiana were to be protected. He regrouped and marched troops 115 miles (185 kilometers) overland to take Fort Bute in Manchac, Louisiana. Amazingly, sources say he won Fort Bute without any further losses of his men.

With the success at Fort Bute behind him, Gálvez marched on to take Baton Rouge. Gálvez knew losing any troops would weaken his whole colony. He knew he needed a way to capture Baton Rouge without sacrificing his men to do so. He had a trick up his sleeve. The forest grew near the fort at Baton Rouge on one side. Gálvez put some of his troops to work in these woods, making an obvious effort to establish a trench and set up to fight. The British took the bait and focused on defending this side of the fort. Meanwhile, secretly, the rest of Gálvez's troops were setting up real trenches and cannons on the other side! By the time the British realized the deception, it was too late. After three hours of attack by Spanish forces, the British leader, Alexander Dickson, surrendered. With the loss of Baton Rouge, Dickson realized he would be completely cut off from the other British ports at Mobile and Pensacola, and he would no longer be able to receive crucial supplies. So he surrendered Fort Natchez without a fight. In total, Gálvez and his troops captured five British forts. Their efforts kept the Mississippi River safe for Spain and the American colonies to continue trade and transportation of supplies and information.

Artist William Salter painted this portrait of British leader Alexander Dickson. Dickson surrendered to Gálvez once he realized that he was surrounded and cut off from further support from Britain.

CHAPTER FOUR

PERSISTENCE AND PENSACOLA

The successful capture of several important forts in the Mississippi region was just the beginning. If Spain was going to protect its claims in the Americas and its power across the globe, it needed the Gulf of Mexico. Mobile, Alabama, and Pensacola, Florida, were key ports. West Florida's location bordering Louisiana Territory threatened Spain.

In January 1780, Gálvez set sail from New Orleans with a fleet of ships destined for Mobile Bay, where they hoped to take control of Fort Charlotte and push the British out of key territory on the way to Pensacola. Once again, the weather played an important role.

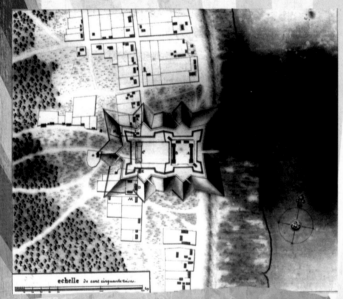

The fort at Mobile, Alabama, would be important for Spain. Gálvez needed to secure Mobile in order to begin overtaking West Florida, a British territory.

A violent storm battered the fleet. Gálvez lost many supplies. He was about to turn back to New Orleans when help arrived and allowed him to press on. It would take until March before all was in order and the Spanish forces would launch their attack on Fort Charlotte. There were more than 700 troops under Gálvez, while only 250 men were defending the fort for the British. Seeing no hope of success, the British commander at Fort Charlotte was forced to surrender on March 13, 1780. No further British forces remained to secure Pensacola. With victory more possible than ever, the final push for Gálvez and Spain would soon be underway.

"YO SOLO"

Months of preparation led Gálvez to Havana, a key Spanish port at the crossroads of the Gulf of Mexico and the Atlantic Ocean. There, he mustered troops for the final battle to push Britain out of the Gulf of Mexico. As he eyed Pensacola, the capital of West Florida, Gálvez knew he would need a vast army to capture the well-guarded city. Pensacola was defended by more than two thousand British soldiers as well as Indians

During Gálvez's campaign for the Gulf Coast, he moved to Havana, an important port in Spain's territory. Havana was filled with cargo and men who could join Gálvez's efforts.

fighting on the British side. The bay was also occupied by British warships guarding the city.

In October, everything was prepared, and Gálvez set out with a flotilla of nearly four thousand troops. But a devastating hurricane season delayed their efforts. Just as the troops set out, further disaster struck. On October 20, 1780, the storm now known as Solano's Hurricane smashed into the fleet with terrifying force.

COAT OF ARMS

A coat of arms is an important symbol of family history. It is also known as a shield of arms or an armorial bearing. In battle, this symbol might be found on a shield or on a flag. These symbols recognize important family connections, history, occupations, or land ownership. A combination of different colors and symbols is used in different locations on the coat of arms in order to express significant messages about the person carrying the shield. These shields and flags could be used to identify the dead in battle or to signify importance and identity between knights and nobles. From medieval times, when many people were unable to read, these bold symbols were one way anyone could recognize important family history and alliances. On a battlefield, being able to recognize a coat of arms could mean knowing the difference between friend and foe—a lifesaving bit of information!

Many of the ships carrying Gálvez's troops were badly damaged and sank. More than half of his troops were lost.

Forced to return to Havana, the initial attack on Pensacola was delayed once again. Gálvez wouldn't quit, however, writing that he wouldn't be deterred by just a storm. For several months, Gálvez reorganized his troops. He arranged for further food and supplies to be brought to Havana to strengthen the will of the men remaining. More men joined his army. When the army and navy were recovered, Gálvez set sail once again, in February.

Arriving in the bay outside Pensacola, Spain prepared to attack. The siege began on March 18, 1781. Gálvez's brilliant

This engraving by Vernier shows the siege of Pensacola. During this key battle of the American Revolution, Gálvez used brilliant planning and strong leadership to secure a win for Spain.

planning and leadership would earn him the inscription "Yo solo" on his coat of arms. "Yo solo" means "I alone," representing his persistence and bravery. His inscription may say, "I alone," but he cared for his troops and successfully led nearly seven thousand men. The battle for Pensacola raged for two months. During that time, Gálvez and his troops suffered losses and hard-

PENSACOLA, THE COASTAL JEWEL

For years, St. Augustine, Florida, held the claim of "oldest city in America." Founded on the Atlantic Ocean by Spanish admiral Pedro Menéndez de Avilés in 1565, St. Augustine still holds the title of oldest continuously lived-in city. However, Pensacola may truly be the oldest European settlement. Researchers have discovered evidence of Pensacola's history from August 1559— six years before St. Augustine was founded. When explorer Tristán de Luna arrived in the bay off what would become Pensacola, he brought African slaves and Mexican craftsmen, bringing multiple cultures to America at the same time. Luna was sure the breathtaking bay and beautiful surrounding lands would be a treasured jewel in Spain's empire. Unfortunately, Luna's luck ran out. A terrible hurricane struck his fleet in September 1559. Many of Luna's ships sank and his resources plummeted. Luna was forced to send many of the survivors to Mexico, leaving just a few soldiers at the Pensacola site. By 1561, these soldiers returned to Mexico. Even with the temporary abandonment of Pensacola, the seeds were planted for a Spanish settlement there. Over the years, Pensacola would develop into a military outpost, then a settlement, and finally a flourishing city. Spain, France, Britain, and Spain once again would lay claim to the diverse city. Cultures would blend and Pensacola would shine on, eventually being signed over to the United States in 1821. Today, the buildings carry echoes of this rich history, with Spanish architectural styles, French influences, and artifacts from British occupation. Historians and archaeologists study the past of this historic place to understand the city that perhaps Luna could only have imagined.

ship. Gálvez himself was wounded in the hand and abdomen by a musket ball, and disease killed other troops. The siege killed seventy-eight Spanish soldiers and nearly two hundred more were injured. Still, Gálvez and his troops pressed on. In May, Spanish forces hit a gunpowder storage area in a Pensacola fort, causing great damage and killing nearly one hundred British loyalists and soldiers. On May 9, 1781, Spain captured Pensacola. Historians call the siege at Pensacola the battle that crippled the British. British troops were spread across the colonies in battle. This Spanish victory meant the British had fewer reinforcements. American Colonial general George Washington readily recognized Gálvez's victory as a key win in turning the tide in favor of the Americans.

CHAPTER FIVE

BAHAMAS AND BEYOND

With the victorious sweep of the Gulf Coast, Gálvez and his diverse military forces changed the balance of power in North America. Once again, Spain claimed lands from the tip of South America northward to Alaska and across the Mississippi into Florida. Great Britain lost West Florida, a colony that had never even rebelled like its northern colonies. Then, in October 1781, American troops under George Washington and its French allies seized Yorktown. British lord Cornwallis surrendered on October 19, ending the last major military conflict of the American Revolution. Spanish success in the Gulf Coast probably influenced Britain's decision after Yorktown to evacuate troops from the colonies. Even so, the greater war for power between Spain, France, and Great Britain continued. Great Britain was losing its powerful hold on the Americas.

With the Gulf Coast secure, Gálvez moved into the Bahamas in May 1782, where he successfully captured a British naval base. This further weakened Great Britain's influence in the region. It seemed there would be no stopping Gálvez. His military strategies and inspiring leadership brought success across the Gulf of Mexico and into the Bahamas and Spanish power in the Americas. Finally, he set his sights on Jamaica, a final stronghold of British control. Instead, Gálvez was called upon to help negotiate peace. He worked with American Benjamin Franklin and other delegates in writing the agreements for peace in the

Treaty of Paris. On September 3, 1783, the Treaty of Paris was signed, officially ending the war. Thanks to Gálvez and his strong leadership, a new, free future was shaped for many people.

RECOVERY AND REWARD

After his efforts to secure a vast territory for the Spanish crown and then to negotiate peace among mighty nations and the new United States of America, Gálvez and his family returned to Spain. King Charles III honored Gálvez for his efforts on behalf of the crown with a title of nobility and promoted him to lieutenant general and governor of not only Louisiana, but West Florida as well. By February 1784, King Charles III titled Gálvez captain general of Cuba.

The Treaty of Paris, shown here, signaled peace between Great Britain, Spain, and the new United States of America. Gálvez was a member of the negotiation team who wrote the treaty.

Arriving in Havana, where he once planned his brilliant victory of Pensacola, Gálvez and his family were welcomed as heroes. His efforts for Spain and the stability of the region continued. He oversaw peace negotiations between Spain and the United States over boundaries in Florida and helped establish trade agreements between the countries along the Mississippi River.

When American merchants were captured in Havana, Gálvez saw that they were released, furthering peace with the young United States. Finally, in 1785, Gálvez was promoted once again. King Charles III named him viceroy of New Spain to succeed his father, who had died in November of 1784.

When Gálvez became viceroy, he and his family moved to Mexico City, at the heart of the Spanish Empire in the Americas. As viceroy, he was a respected and well-loved leader. Upon his arrival, Mexico City was struggling in a time of famine and disease. Always caring for the people, Gálvez used his own family fortunes, as well as money he secured from the crown, to support the people of New Spain as needed. Buildings that had fallen into disrepair were rebuilt, including the castle of Chapultepec. Gálvez also oversaw the completion of the Cathedral of Mexico. It seemed Gálvez and his young family were destined for the long-lasting favor of the people and success in their endeavors. However, in November 1786, Viceroy Gálvez fell ill. He died on November 30, 1786, at only forty years old. Loved by the people, his body was buried with his father's in a church in San Fernando, but

After aiding America and Spain in the war, Gálvez was promoted to viceroy and he moved to Mexico City with his family, where he was a beloved leader.

COLONIAL NEW SPAIN, ARCHITECTURE

Spain has a long influence in the Americas. From as early as 1519, with the arrival of Hernán Cortés, conquistadors and explorers introduced the Americas to Spanish culture and style. Mexico, specifically Mexico City, became the center of this vast territory under the Spanish crown. Mexico City is home to many buildings in the Spanish architectural style. Some structures use local materials, such as adobe, in their building and are simple, one-level structures. Others are more elaborate, with elegant carvings on the fronts of the buildings. Many homes were built surrounding courtyards within the houses, which was a common style in Spain and the Mediterranean. One glittering example of Spanish influence in architecture in the Americas is the Cathedral of Mexico. This building, the largest and oldest cathedral in the Americas, was started in 1567, but took until the late 1700s to see completion. Inspired by architecture from Spain, the cathedral has statues, pillars, a dome, and bell towers. Inside, typical of other cathedrals in this area and from this era, are statues, multiple altars, paintings, and catacombs underneath. A tour of lands once under Spanish influence, from Florida to the West Coast and south into Mexico, would reveal the influences of the colonial era.

his heart was placed in an urn in Cathedral Mexico, as tribute. Gálvez had poured his life and heart into strengthening an empire in the New World and, with it, had helped the United States of America rise up in independence as well.

A 231-YEAR PROMISE

American independence had been won by the hard work and determination of men and women across the colonies and

Teresa Valcarce is known as the Portrait Lady for her efforts to see this portrait of Gálvez hung in the US Capitol.

beyond. Pollock recalled the efforts of the Louisiana governor who had gone on to become viceroy of New Spain. He sent a portrait of Gálvez to the new Continental Congress (the governing body that would determine what shape the young country would take). Elias Boudinot, the president of the congress, acknowledged the portrait and promised Pollock that it would hang in a congressional meeting room to give Gálvez the honor he deserved. And yet, congress was brand new. There was no capitol building. In fact, there was no capital! Washington, D.C., wouldn't be founded as the nation's capital until 1790. For a time, the portrait hung in a meetinghouse rented for the congressional gatherings. From there, it was moved to Boudinot's home. Despite the glory and gratitude the young country owed Gálvez, the portrait faded from attention. The promise to honor Gálvez was forgotten until 2014. It was then that Teresa Valcarce of Málaga, Spain, caught wind of the portrait and its unfulfilled destiny. Working relentlessly to pressure congress, Valcarce's efforts paid off. After plenty of pressure on various members, a Gálvez portrait now hangs in a committee room in the US Capitol. After 231 years, Gálvez was even granted honorary citizenship. This is an appropriate tribute for a man who gave so much to the cause of freedom and the birth of the nation that now honors him.

TIMELINE

1746 Bernardo de Gálvez born to Matías and Josepha Madrid y Gallardo de Gálvez in Málaga, Spain.

1762 Gálvez serves in Portugal for the Royal Spanish Army and is promoted to captain.

1770 Gálvez is put in command of New Spain's northern territory against Apache warriors.

1771 Gálvez is wounded in the Pecos and Gila River area in expeditions against the Apache.

1772 Gálvez returns to Spain and moves to France to work with the Regiment of Cantabria.

1775 He is assigned to the Regiment of Seville and leads an unsuccessful campaign in Algeria and is wounded.

1776 The Declaration of Independence is signed on July 4, stating American colonial separation from Great Britain. Gálvez is transferred to the Louisiana Territory.

1777 Gálvez is promoted to governor of Louisiana on January 1.

He marries Félicité de Saint-Maxent d'Estréhan.

He begins smuggling supplies to American troops.

1779 Gálvez is promoted to brigadier general. Spain declares war on Great Britain in June. The Battle for New Orleans in fought in August.

1779–1782 Gálvez arranges for an estimated ten to fifteen thousand cattle to be rounded up and driven to the troops in order to feed the army he mustered.

1781 Gálvez leads the siege of Pensacola in March. The siege lasts until May 8, when Pensacola falls under Spanish control. The British Royal Army surrenders at Yorktown on October 19.

1783 Gálvez returns to Spain after his victory in the Bahamas; he remains there until 1784.

1784 Gálvez is recalled to serve as captain-general and governor of Cuba.

1785 He represents Spain in negotiations with the United States regarding the territory of Florida between Spain and the United States. On June 17, he arrives in Mexico City for his duties as the newly appointed viceroy.

1786 Gálvez dies of illness in New Spain.

2014 The portrait of Gálvez, long promised to hang in the US Capitol, is finally placed in December.

GLOSSARY

ally A state or country formally cooperating with another for military or economic gain.

arms Weapons and supplies for military groups.

campaign A military move or series of moves in order to achieve a particular goal.

coat of arms A shield, or image of a shield, used to represent a family's history and achievements.

emissary A person sent on a special mission.

famine An extreme food shortage leading to widespread hunger or starvation.

flotilla A group of ships or boats working toward the same activity under one leadership.

frontier The farthest boundary of settled land on the border of a country.

hostility Acts of war, unfriendliness, or opposition.

independence The state of self-government or self-rule in a country.

intelligence Information used to help military or government leaders make decisions.

negotiations Talks intended for resolving conflict or disagreement.

patriot An American colonist in favor of independence from Great Britain.

rebel A person who is acting in resistance to a government or leader.

regiment A unit of a military branch that is controlled by a particular leader.

representation Elected leaders chosen to speak for the people who selected them, such as in Parliament or Congress.

resolution A formal decision to do or not do something.

revolution The overthrow of a government in order to establish a new one.

rival A person or country competing against another.

smuggle Moving goods, supplies, or information from one place to another secretly.

tax Money required to be given to a government, usually taken from sales of goods or income.

treaty A formal agreement between two countries.

urn A special vase or container used to hold the remains of a person.

viceroy A ruler acting in a colony for the interests of a supreme ruler, such as a monarch.

FOR MORE INFORMATION

Canadian Museum of History
100 Laurier Street
Gatineau, QC K1A 0M8
Canada
Website: http://www
    .historymuseum.ca
Facebook: @CaMusHistory
Twitter: @CanMusHistory
The Canadian Museum of
    History offers a broader look
    at the issues leading up to
    the American Revolution,
    including the fur trade, New
    France, and the colonial era
    in Canada.

Canadian War Museum
1 Vimy Place
Ottawa, ON K1A 0M8
Canada
(800) 555-5621
Website: http://www
    .warmuseum.ca
Twitter: @CanWarMuseum
Facebook: @WarMuseum
The Canadian War Museum
    covers the history of
    Canada's military involve-
    ment in the world. Coverage
    of the American Revolution
    includes a fresh perspective
    on the American loyal-

ists' migration to Canada
in 1783 and the invasion
of American troops into
Canada in 1775 to 1776.

Florida Historical Society
435 Brevard Avenue
Cocoa, FL 32922
(321) 690-1971
Website: https://
    myfloridahistory.org
Facebook:
    @FloridaHistoricalSociety
YouTube: @myFloridaHistory
The Florida Historical Society
    serves to preserve and
    share the history of Florida.
    Florida's history is inter-
    twined with the history of
    colonial France, Spain, and
    Great Britain and the era of
    the American Revolution.

Museum of America
Reyes Católicos Avenue, 6
28040 Madrid, Spain
Telephones: 91 549 26 41
Website: https://www.mecd
    .gob.es/museodeamerica
Facebook: @MuseodeAmerica
YouTube:
    @MadridMuseodeAmerica

The Museum of America houses both collections of pre-Columbian artifacts as well as artifacts and art related to the viceroyalty period of Spain's history in the Americas.

Museum of the American Revolution

101 South Third Street
Philadelphia, PA 19106
(215) 253-6731
Website: https://www
.amrevmuseum.org
Facebook and Twitter:
@amrevmuseum
The Museum of the American Revolution has both online and in-person educational materials covering a wide range of events, ideas, and people of the American Revolution.

National Museum of Viceroyalty

Plaza Hidalgo Number 99,
Barrio San Martín
Tepotzotlán, México
C.P. 54600
58 76 02 45/27 70/92 12

Website: http://www.virreinato
.inah.gob.mx
Facebook: @virreinato
Twitter: @Virreinato
The National Museum of Viceroyalty highlights the culture, art, and history of Mexico and the colonial era in New Spain.

University of West Florida Historic Trust

20 Church Street
Pensacola, FL 32502
(850) 595-5985
Website: http://www
.historicpensacola.org
Facebook and Twitter:
@historicpcola
The University of West Florida Historic Trust provides information about Pensacola's diverse history and the people who shaped it.

FOR FURTHER READING

Fesser, Guillermo. *Getting to Know Bernardo de Gálvez.* Doral, FL: Santillana USA Publishing, 2017.

Hamilton, John. *Final Years of the American Revolution.* ABDO & Daughters, 2013.

Kudlinski, Kathleen V. *Rebel with a Cause: The Daring Adventure of Dicey Langston, Girl Spy of the American Revolution.* North Mankato, MN: Capstone Press, Encounter, 2016.

Lanser, Amanda. *The American Revolution by the Numbers.* North Mankato, MN: Capstone Press, 2016.

Lowery, Zoe. *The American Revolution.* New York, NY: Britannica Educational Publishing, 2016.

Matthews, Rupert. *Conquistadors: History's Fearless Fighters.* New York, NY: Gareth Stevens, 2015.

Nichols, Susan. *Conquistadors.* New York, NY: Britannica Educational Publishing, 2017.

Raum, Elizabeth. *A Revolutionary War Timeline.* North Mankato, MN: Capstone Press Smithsonian, 2014.

Sebastian, Emily. *Colonial and Postcolonial Latin America and the Caribbean.* New York, NY: Britannica Educational Publishing, 2017.

Webb, Sarah Elizabeth. *A Primary Source History of the American Revolution.* North Mankato, MN: Capstone Press, 2016.

BIBLIOGRAPHY

Buescher, John. "Spain in the American Revolution." Teaching History. Retrieved December 30, 2017. http://teachinghistory .org/history-content/ask-a-historian/22894.

Buescher, John. "Spanish Louisiana vs. Great Britain." Teaching History. Retrieved December 30, 2017. http://teachinghistory .org/history-content/ask-a-historian/23456.

Butler, Judge Edward, Sr. "Spain's Involvement in the American Revolutionary War." Granaderos. Retrieved January 25, 2018. www.granaderos.org.

Chamberlain, Charles, and Lo Faber. "Spanish Colonial Louisiana: Encyclopedia of Louisiana." Louisiana Endowment for the Humanities, February 7, 2014. www.knowlouisiana.org.

Cox, Dale. "Battle of Fort Charlotte." Explore Southern History, 2014. http://www.exploresouthernhistory.com/fortcharlotte .html.

de Varona, Frank. *Bernardo de Gálvez*. Milwaukee, WI: Raintree Publishers, 1990.

du Val, Kathleen. *Independence Lost: Lives on the Edge of the American Revolution*. New York, NY: Random House, 2015.

Elliot, John Huxtable. *Empires of the Atlantic World: Britain and Spain in America, 1492–1830*. New Haven, CT: Yale University Press, 2006.

Encyclopedia Britannica editors. "Louisiana Purchase." Encyclopedia Britannica, February 17, 2017. https://www .britannica.com/event/Louisiana-Purchase.

Encyclopedia Britannica editors. "The Viceroyalty of New Spain." Encyclopedia Britannica, May 31, 2013. https://www .britannica.com/place/Viceroyalty-of-New-Spain.

Ferreiro, Larrie D. *Brothers at Arms: American Independence and the Men of France and Spain Who Saved It*. New York, NY: Knopf Publishing, 2016.

Glickstein, Don. *After Yorktown: The Final Struggle for American Independence.* Yardley, PA: Westholme Publishing, 2015.

Herrera, Juan Felipe. *Portraits of Hispanic American Heroes.* New York, NY: Penguin Group USA, 2014.

Hogarth, Frederick, and Leslie Gilbert Pine. "Heraldry." Encyclopedia Britannica, January 12, 2018. https://www.britannica.com/topic/heraldry.

Mitchell, Barbara A. "America's Spanish Savior: Bernardo de Gálvez." History Net, November 28, 2012. http://www.historynet.com/americas-spanish-savior-bernardo-de-galvez.htm.

NOAA. "235th Anniversary of Solano's Hurricane." NOAA/Atlantic Oceanographic and Meteorological Laboratory Hurricane Research Division, October 20, 2015. https://noaahrd.wordpress.com/2015/10/20/235th-anniversary-of-solanos-hurricane.

Pasquier, Michael T. "Bernardo de Gálvez: Encyclopedia of Louisiana." Louisiana Endowment for the Humanities, August 18, 2011. http://www.knowlouisiana.org/entry/bernardo-de-glvez.

Thayer, Bill. "Bernardo de Gálvez Diary." *Louisiana Historical Quarterly*, November 16, 2014. http://penelope.uchicago.edu/Thayer/E/Gazetteer/Places/America/United_States/Louisiana/_Texts/LHQ/1/1/Galvez_Diary*.html.

Thonhoff, Robert. "Bernardo de Galvez." Handbook of Texas Online, September 28, 2016. http://www.tshaonline.org/handbook/online/articles/fga10.

Thonhoff, Robert. "The Life and Times of Bernardo de Gálvez, Spain's Great Hero of the American Revolution." La Revista Online. Retrieved February 8, 2018. www.granaderos.org.

Webster, Donovan. "Harboring History in Pensacola."
    Smithsonian, May 2009.https://www.smithsonianmag.com
    /travel/harboring-history-in-pensacola-125617869.
Weddle, Robert S. "Gálvez Crossings on the Pecos River."
    Handbook of Texas Online, June 15, 2010. http://www
    .tshaonline.org/handbook/online/articles/rkgdz.

INDEX

ABOUT THE AUTHOR

Michelle McIlroy is a New York State certified teacher with fifteen years' experience in a fifth-grade classroom. She has written curriculum focusing on the voices less often heard in our traditional history curriculum and encourages her readers to think critically. She has also written a biography about Holocaust resistance fighter Sophie Scholl. McIlroy lives and writes from her farmhouse in upstate New York.

PHOTO CREDITS